Presented to

_____

By

_____

Date

_____

Occasion

_____

_____

HOW HE GOT ME STARTED

HOW HE GOT ME STARTED

AMAZING LIFE STORIES OF THE
POWER OF GOD LIKE IN BIBLE TIMES

Luc Nounagnon

Sofer Publishing

How He Got Me Started
Amazing Life Stories Of The Power Of God Like In Bible Times

Copyright © 2024 Luc Nounagnon

All rights reserved. No part of this book may be reproduced or transmitted in any form or by any means, electronic or mechanical, including photocopying, recording, or by any information storage and retrieval system, without written permission from the author.

ISBN: 979-8-9909092-0-5 (Hardback)
ISBN: 9781736221785 (Paperback)
ISBN: 978-1-7362217-9-2 (eBook)
ISBN: 979-8-9909092-1-2 (Audio Book)

For more information, please contact:
Sofer Publishing, LLC,
Herndon, VA 20171, USA
contact@soferpublishing.com
https://soferpublishing.com/

All New Testament quotations, unless otherwise indicated, are taken from *The Chronological Gospels, The Life and Seventy-Week Ministry of the Messiah*, Second Edition. Copyright © 2023 by Michael John Rood. Used by permission of Michael John Rood. All rights reserved worldwide.

Scripture quotations marked CJB are taken from the *Complete Jewish Bible*, Copyright © 1998 and 2016 by David H. Stern. Used by Permission of Messianic Jewish Publishers, www.messianicjewish.net. All rights reserved worldwide.

Sofer Publishing

Disclaimer

Disclaimer 1: All characters appearing in this book are real. Any resemblance to actual persons, living and dead, is purely based on truth. The scripture in this book is the true, inspired Word of Yehovah God the Creator. As a contribution to the ongoing efforts to share more light on the Hebrew roots of our Christian Faith, the true name of God of Abraham, Isaac, and Israel, with its recovered consonants that help its correct reading, has been used throughout this work as YeHoVah. For more information, please check the works of Nehemia Gordon and Michael Rood on the subject. In the same understanding, the Hebrew name of our Savior, "Yeshua" has been used along with 'Jesus Christ' in the book.

Disclaimer 2: The reader is fully responsible for any action he or she may take because of this sharing. Medical doctors, Medicine and medication still have their role to play and can go as far as a person of faith allows them.

Dedication

I dedicate this book to the full author of its content, that is, to Holy Spirit, to Yeshua and to Yehovah God Almighty who created all things seen and unseen. To you be *all* the glory from generation to generation and forevermore!

Acknowledgments

I would like to express my sincere gratitude and love to my wife and our children who moved Holy Spirit to instruct me to put in writing what He did through me that they were enjoying hearing so much. A big thank you Holy Spirit for all that you did through me that you want others to also read, hear and enjoy.

I thank Yehovah God for the lives of all of you, whose names are mentioned or not mentioned in this book but had contributed or shared in all the awesome events narrated in this book. Yehovah, our God Almighty, the Ancient of Days make you prosper in every way, in the supreme and glorious name of Yeshua our Savior.

Foreword

I started reading this book the first time, with great expectations. Recently, the author, my husband, had been sharing with our children every Shabbat (Saturday), snippets of the things Holy Spirit did through him. I could recall the ones that I had lived through or that he had shared with me. However, I did not know all of them.

What I did not expect was to go through the entire book in a single seating. Realizing how passionate I was reading this book full of acts of Holy Spirit, my husband asked if I would not want to take a break. I ignored him the first time and kept reading, because at last, I had the opportunity to read the whole "series". He insisted that I take a break, to which I shouted with a smile on my face, "No! Let me see the end of this part; I cannot stop mid-way. I am just on Part 2-D!". He jokingly replied, "You want to see the end now? There is no C after D! How will you 'see' after D?" I laughed and decided to make it my foreword short story.

Each book has its own "taste"! *'This one, taste and see!'* It has the "virtue" to keep the reader captivated from cover to cover! You have been "fore-warned"; pun-intended!

In truth, what keeps you captivated is the wonder world of the works of Holy Spirit. You learn that if you make yourself available through a life of Holiness in our modern days, Holy Spirit's power is still available, doing all the acts that we read in the Bible from Yeshua to the Apostles. This, regardless of the limitations that denominations and doctrines have disseminated in the Church.

Therefore, if you are a young girl or boy looking for a path that can help you build up your relationship and commitment to your Savior and Master Yeshua (Jesus Christ), this book is for you. Similarly, if you are an adult who wants the same thing as the youth or have questions regarding the works of Holy Spirit, this book is absolutely yours as well. Finally, if you have been in the church and looking for an inspiration to catch "fire" from Holy Spirit, you have just been served!

D. Nounagnon, Ph. D.

Preface

How did the book come about? In the calm of the night of April 1, 2024, I heard inside of me the voice of Holy Spirit saying, "Write them in a book". I responded, "What shall I write in a book?" the same voice responded, "What I did through you that you have been sharing with the kids."

A joy filled my heart, and a smile came on my face. I grabbed my notebook and began writing. Almost all the events that I shared in this book and that took place in Chicago, happened while I was still in my very early thirties.

Before that night of April 1st, every Shabbat, I had been sharing these events a little bit at a time with my children and wife. The kids were so excited to hear more. However, at the end of each short story, I gave them an appointment on the following Shabbat. This happened through the entire month of March. None of our five (5) children had experienced these events, if not just one. Although the three (3) oldest were on the family trip with us to Switzerland early 2020, they did not share in the exciting moment of the move of Holy Spirit. They were in the children ministry area. My wife experienced some of the events after our marriage.

Now that we have a family with kids growing older, this sharing sounds a lot like a team build-up. We will soon see what Yeshua has for us together as a family!

To Yehovah God Almighty, To Yeshua His Holy Lamb who defeated the Adversary and redeemed all humanity and creation for His Father, and To Holy Spirit our guide and Comforting Counselor be all the glory and honor and power from generation to generation and forevermore!

Contents

Dedication ix
Acknowledgments xi
Foreword xiii
Preface xv
Contents xvii
Introduction 1
I While Living In Benin 3
  A *Committed To Yeshua For A Life Of Sanctification* 5
  B *Fell Sick To Death But Trusted Only Yeshua To Heal Him* . . . 9
  C *Prayed And Fire "Came Down"* 13
  D *Confronted A Demon-Possessed In A Street* 17
  E *Prayed and His Brother Recovered His Sight* 21
II While Living In The United States Of America 23
  A *Prayed And Closed A Psychic Business In Chicago* 25
  B *Was Sick To Death Again And Trusted Yeshua To Heal Him* . 29
  C *Las Vegas Versus Yeshua* 33
  D *Prayed Over The Phone And Holy Spirit "Beat Up" A Brother* 39
  E *Prayed For The Gift Of Visions But Was Anointed Prophet* . . 45
  F *Proclaimed Prophet In Three Instances Over Two Continents* . 47

G	*Slapped A Demon And It Sounded Like A Thousand Thunders*	57
H	*Chased A Demon-Possessed Out Of A Church*	61
I	*Prayed And Closed Another Psychic Business*	65
J	*Prayed And A Sound System Was Fixed Live*	67
K	*Turned To Look At A Gay, And Two Of Them Ran Off*	71
L	*Prayed For A Man And The Wife Almost Called The Police* .	75
M	*Immersed in Water and Could No Longer Speak And Eat* ..	81
N	*A Teaser Of Speaking In Tongues Spoke In Tongues*	87
O	*Stretched Out His Hand And A Lady Was Lifted Off The Ground*	91
P	*Pointed His Finger And Decorative Angels Disappeared*	95
Q	*A "Sick And Blind" Donation Almost Killed A Brother*	99
R	*Spoke In Tongues In His Sleep And Fell Twice From The Bed* .	103
S	*Got Help Twice From Angels In International Airports*	105
T	*Caught Up In Heavenly Realm And Heard Angels Praising Yehovah*	115
III	While Visiting Switzerland And Benin	119
A	*Switzerland 2020*	121
B	*Benin 2021*	125
IV	End Notes....................................	129
	End notes....................................	131
	About the Author	139

¹⁵ *And said again God to Moses, thus you shall say to the sons of Israel,* יְהֹוָה *the God of your fathers, the God of Abraham, the God of Isaac, and the God of Jacob has sent me to you; this (is) My name forever, and this (is) My title to generation of generation.*

Exo.3v15
The Interlinear Bible: Hebrew-Greek-English
by Jay P. Green, Sr. (Literal translation)
Printed in the USA - Jan. 2022

Introduction

In this book, the author will take you through numerous exciting events he experienced with Yeshua the Mashiach (Jesus Christ), from adolescence to adulthood in North America, Europe, and Africa. You will read how the power of Holy Spirit worked in several unpredictable circumstances. You will read about miraculous healing. You will read about the benefits of sanctification. You will read about speaking in tongues, slapping demons, Holy Spirit "beating up" someone. You will read about praying to close deceitful businesses. The list is endless. At the end, you will either praise Yehovah God and Yeshua His Holy Lamb or wonder what it means to be saved. So, buckle up! And enjoy the ride!

Part I

While Living In Benin

A

Committed To Yeshua For A Life Of Sanctification

This commitment happened in three gradual phases while I was still a teenager. The *first phase* was at home when I used to watch our mother display hostilities towards most girls who came around my elder bothers. She used to say, "Boys, your education first. If you get a girl pregnant now, you are 'screwed'!" One day a school mate, a girl, paid me a surprise visit. After she left, my dad sat me down and said, "Son, it is not always for schoolwork that some girls hang around some boys. There could be more to it. If you get trapped, you could ruin the dreams of your life. Teen pregnancy is a dangerous thing". I took good note of that advice.

The *second phase* was at church. I attended a youth meeting about living a Christ-centered life. At the conclusion of the meeting, we were asked to make an individual commitment to Christ. During that quiet moment of self-examination and decision making, I remembered the words of my parents. I made the decision not to have sexual relations before marriage. Even with my fiancée. By the grace of Yehovah, I held onto my commitment, although I was challenged over time and kissed some girls along the way. The "voice" of that commitment was speaking to me and kept me from compromising situations. Whenever needed, it will remind me that I had committed to a life of purity.

The *third phase* was not long after the second one started. I decided to avoid telling lies; "big and small". Before this decision, I had defined in my own understanding some categorizations of lie in big lies and small lies. Through that self-defined system of appreciation, I used to calm the challenging voice of my conscience or what is called spirit of man.

I also, decided not to drink alcohol or liquor. I was not a drinker of alcohol before, even though I did taste beer prior to this decision. The fact that my parents used to drink only occasionally when they had some visitors or during some celebrations, made this decision much easier. Growing up in the Protestant Methodist Church, there was no teaching emphasizing living a life of sanctification. Even during events that gathered multiple congregations, there was no such teaching. It is unfortunate when you consider the reality that the founders of Methodism, namely John Wesley, Charles Wesley and George Whitefield, started with sanctified life living in the Holy Club movement.

How *He* Got Me Started

¹⁵ *On the contrary, following the Holy One who called you, become **holy yourselves in your entire way of life**;* ¹⁶ *since the Tanakh says, "You are to be holy because I am holy."*

1 Pet. 1v15-16 (CJB)

⁴⁴ *For I am* יְהֹוָה *your God; therefore,* ***consecrate yourselves and be holy****, for I am holy; and do not defile yourselves with any kind of swarming creature that moves along the ground.*

Lev. 11v44

² *"Speak to the entire community of Isra'el; tell them, '**You people are to be holy** because I,* יְהֹוָה *your God, am holy."*

Lev. 19v2

⁸ *Observe my regulations and obey them; I am* יְהֹוָה*,* ***who sets you apart to be holy****.*

Lev. 20v8

B

Fell Sick To Death But Trusted Only Yeshua To Heal Him

Note: *The reader is* fully *responsible for any action he or she may take because of this sharing. Medical doctors, Medicine and medication still have their role to play and can go as far as a person of faith allows them.*

This event happened while I was 16 or 17 years old. I attended the wedding reception of a cousin. It was on the rooftop, on the 4th floor of a building near the beach. I was among the first to arrive on the site. I was around enjoying the beautiful view of the Atlantic Ocean from the top. After a little while, I started shivering. I suddenly felt so sick that I had to be rushed home for care. I refused any treatment my parents were giving me. I told them that Yeshua (it was Jesus then) whom they introduced to me is also a healer, I read. I trusted Him to heal me. After three days of no improvement, my parents offered to take me to the hospital. I opposed that decision. Alarmed by my condition, my mother asked a doctor (a female cousin) to come check me at home. She came the next day. She was also a member of the Protestant Methodist Church like my family. She diagnosed an acute malaria. For what is known, malaria is a serious life-threatening disease. It was already a week, and I was still laying in bed and could only get up to use the toilet. I had no desire for water or food and could hardly keep in any little food I tried to eat.

She recommended that my parents take me to a hospital immediately. I opposed it and told her that the Yeshua I learned about in church should and must heal me. Seeing my stubbornness, she warned me of playing with sudden death. She gave me some anti-malaria pills to take on the spot. I refused to take them. She became very furious. However, knowing how much she cares for my mom and our family, I took the medication from her hand but refused to put any in my mouth.

Once she left the room, I dropped them on the nightstand. The "I trust you to heal me" showdown continued for about two more days. Then, I experienced a very scary moment. It was when I needed to go to the toilet (only urinating) and almost fell. I was so frail, weak, and in deep pain. I hardly held on. I thought at that moment that I was about to die! But I spoke to myself, saying, "I'm not afraid to die. Yeshua will heal me." I went back to my bed and fell in a very deep sleep for long hours. I could not remember exactly for how long I slept until my mother woke me up with another hot and spicy meal. Once awake, this time, I felt strength in my bones! Praise Yehovah! I felt very good as well. No more headache! No more pain! All those manifestations had vanished! Praise Yehovah! I left the meal and took a good shower! I had not showered for more than ten (10) days. My mother only rubbed my body with a warm piece of

How *He* Got Me Started

cloth.

Praise Yehovah for our virtuous mothers in Yeshua! Yes indeed! Yeshua had healed me! That was it! It was done! I had demonstrated my victory over sickness and death through trusting Yeshua! I have learnt that as believer in Yeshua, if you are not afraid to die, you will live. I did it again years later when Satan threw another sickness punch at me in Chicago, in the US. This time, while I was alone in a far land. And of course, you can image how it ended. After those two deadly attacks long years ago, Satan tried it again in September 2023 by a direct death spirit attack during my sleep (in my dream). I saw blood gushing out of my mouth while my arms were getting paralyzed. Of course, you can imagine how it ended. Praise Yehovah!

C

Prayed And Fire "Came Down"

This event happened mid-1999 at a retreat of the young Christian community that I was leading. On the second day of the retreat, there was a common understanding that irrespective of the good preparation, the power of Holy Spirit was not flowing. We understood that there were some attacks coming from some strongholds of the Adversary in the neighborhood. To "clear the air", we split in small groups and went on prayers of counterattacks. During this prayer in my group, I asked to pray that the fire of God come down and burn any altar that is standing against the success of our retreat. So, we did. In the middle of the prayer, it started raining with thunder flashing through the sky. A bit later, the rain stopped, and the intercession prayers concluded. We went on a break. Some participants went for a walk outside of the retreat site. To my surprise, some of them returned in rush to call me. They wanted me to go outside and see what happened in a house nearby. They said, "We prayed for fire against evil altars and indeed the fire came down!" For a quick moment I had forgotten that prayer request.

Outside, I saw a crowd near a house with its sidewall busted. I noticed a couple of fire fighters' vehicles on standby. I was told that a resident of the house was praying with a candle when the house caught fire; a statement that corroborated the thesis of some of my prayer group members. From that afternoon, the retreat took off like a rocket. The fire of Holy Spirit was lit! Praise be to Yehovah God Almighty and to His Holy Lamb Yeshua our Savior! It is worth mentioning that my father was also at this retreat. He attended along with some members of a new Christian community that he joined after leaving the Protestant Methodist Church. This was a time when the Protestant Methodist Church of Benin was resisting the message of new birth and the Pentecostal experience with speaking in tongues. It was a very sad reality.

How *He* Got Me Started

¹*Now about that time King Herod began to persecute particular members of the Kehila...* ¹²*He was still pondering these things when he arrived at the house of Miriam, the mother of Yochanan (whose surname was Marcus), where many were gathered together praying...* ²¹*Upon a set day, Herod, who was arrayed in his royal apparel, sat upon his throne and made a speech to them.* ²²*The people gave a shout, saying, "It is the voice of a mighty god, not of a man."* ²³*Immediately the angel of* יְהֹוָה *smote him because he did not give the glory to* יְהֹוָה *and he was devoured by worms and died.* ²⁴*The word of* יְהֹוָה *grew and multiplied.*

Acts 12v1-24

Kehila: Messianic Community.

D

Confronted A Demon-Possessed In A Street

This event took place early 1999 on a Friday while I was still working in the financial sector. I could remember the day because I used to fast and pray every Friday. At lunch break, after spending some time in prayer in my office, I walked outside of the building to refresh myself. Although it is a crowded business street by default, I noticed an unusual rushing flow of pedestrians and bikers coming from the opposing direction. As I raised my eyes to see what was causing the scene, I noticed a demon-possessed man in the middle of the street disrupting the traffic. He was going left and right threatening both pedestrians and bikers. Cars had to stop. For a quick moment, I wondered if I should look for safety like everyone else was doing. Then inside of me I heard, "You just prayed, right? Let's see if Yeshua can chase these demons." I understood it was the voice of the Adversary. Thus, I replied, "Really! Let's go for it"!

I strengthened my walk and continued moving forward on the same sidewalk, not changing direction, while keeping an eye on the man. Then, our eyes crossed. The demon-possessed man jumped from the middle of the street to my side of the sidewalk. He started walking toward me half-bent forward as to leap at me. I continued walking toward him with my eyes fixated on his. I did not utter a single word. When we were about six (6) feet apart, I saw in his eyes that fear had seized him.

    He calmly stepped from the sidewalk. Then, he hid behind a parked car that he began to use as a buffer between us. His eyes were watching every single move I was making, while walking away from me. Once he felt safe enough, he ran off. Praise God! I continued my walk as if nothing happened, leaving speechless some from the crowd who must be wondering, what just happened. But I know who I am! A moving dwelling of Yeshua who defeated Satan about two thousand years ago. Praise be to Yehovah our God, from generation to generation and forevermore!

How *He* Got Me Started

¹³ *Then certain itinerant Jewish exorcists took it upon themselves to speak the name of Messiah Yeshua over those who had demonic spirits, saying, "We command you by Yeshua whom Shaul preaches." ...* ¹⁵ *The evil spirit answered them, "Yeshua I know, and Shaul I know, but who are you?* ¹⁶ *The man who was possessed by the demon leaped on them, overcame them, and prevailed against them, so that they fled out of the house naked and wounded.*

Acts 19v13-16

E Prayed and His Brother Recovered His Sight

This event took place in our family home. One early morning my younger brother left his bed to use the toilet. I noticed that he was not walking right, and his eyes were still closed. On his return I held him back and realized that he could not talk, and his eyes were fully closed. However, he could hear me and react. But he had lost his speech and his sight.

I used the palm of my hands to flip his eyes opened. Still, he could not see. His eyes closed back immediately. I made him seat and called an uncle that was living with us. I prayed and laid hands on him. He recovered his speech, and his eyes were opened. He could speak and see again. He still does. Praise Yehovah our God!

Part II

While Living In The United States Of America

A

Prayed And Closed A Psychic Business In Chicago

It was 2001. I was still a newcomer to America, when this event happened. There was a psychic lady that had a live divination show on TV. Her clients used to call-in live. I did not like to see her on my screen. So, for some time, my solution was to switch channels. Still, I was not satisfied. It was my TV after all! Thank God, she finally made the mistake of emailing a sister, telling her things about "her star" and providing her with a phone number to call for more information. Informed, I became angry. I took the phone number, prayed on it, and then called.

Once she was finally over the line, I asked if she is the one. She confirmed! I told her not to hang up! I started praying in tongues against her and her demons. This went on for about twenty minutes. When I was done, her line was still opened. Then I hung up. About two (2) to three (3) weeks later, the news reported that the TV psychic lady of Chicago was found guilty of multiple accusations in the courthouse and sent to jail. Halleluyah! Her psychic business was taken off the air. For the following ten (10) years, I neither saw her on a TV network in Chicago, nor heard of her again. Praise be to Yehovah our God, for His love and for giving us through Yeshua power over deceitful businesses as well.

How *He* Got Me Started

16 It came to pass, as we went to prayer, that we met a servant girl possessed with a spirit of divination, which brought her masters much profit by fortune-telling. ... 18 ... Finally, Shaul, being grieved, turned and said to the spirit, "I command you in the name of Yeshua Messiah, come out of her!" The demonic spirit came out immediately. 19 When her masters saw that their hope of profiting from her was gone, they took hold of Shaul and Silas and brought them to the captains of the marketplace.

Acts 16v16-19

B

Was Sick To Death Again And Trusted Yeshua To Heal Him

Note: *The reader is* fully *responsible for any action he or she may take because of this sharing. Medical doctors, Medicine and medication still have their role to play and can go as far as a person of faith allows them.*

This second deadly attack through my health happened at the end of June 2000, less than a year after my arrival in the US. I just had a career change from banking to Telecom. All of us new recruits went through a week of training that concluded on a Thursday afternoon. On my way home, I suddenly felt sick and was losing control of myself. I rushed home, dropped my bag, threw off my jacket and went into prayer. I prayed for hours until I couldn't go on any longer. On the contrary, I felt worse. As it was getting dark, I heard a voice inside of me saying, "You are about to die. Call the ambulance or call 911 police emergency line." I refused and replied that my healer is in the apartment with me. Nevertheless, I grew weaker and could not get off the floor. A deep pain invaded all my being and did not let go until the next day. I had just a little bit of sleep.

The second night was at hand. I continued trusting only Yeshua to heal and restore me. Then I heard a voice inside me again saying, "Remember that you are alone in this apartment. Tonight, you will die. Call 911." At that point I decided to do something radical. I reached out to a piece of paper and grabbed a pen. With the little strength left in me, I wrote "I trust Yeshua (Jesus Christ) to heal me". I dropped that disclaimer on my coffee table in the living room where I had been laying on the floor for the second night. I wrote that note to help explain what happened in case Yeshua had changed his mind about healing me. I spent the second night on the floor in pain. All day Saturday I was on the floor, weak and in pain. During that third (3rd) night, I gathered my strength and crawled into my bedroom and into my bed. The carpet floor was not helping the pain in my body. I was still in my work outfit, except the jacket. I did not know that I was about to live the most terrifying night of my life to date. All my prayers were reduced to "Yeshua, I trust you to heal me as you did in Benin". Once in bed, I prayed to have an instant deep sleep of rest. It happened. But not for long. A violent headache grabbed hold of me and the pain shot through my entire body. It was crushing. It did not let go till the following morning. The pain and its violence were such that they caused me to roll back and forth in my bed and fall. I fell from the bed three times that night and each time I pulled myself back up. I refused to stay on the floor.

On Sunday morning, the rolling stopped. However, I was still in serious pain and very weak. I do not even remember having used the toilet since the attack started. My prayer and deep conviction had not changed. However, my situation was about to change! Halleluyah! Early Sunday afternoon, suddenly, I felt a relief. I was able to seat down on my bed for the first time since Thursday afternoon. I stood and did not fall. I stretched my arms and took a few steps and did not fall. I bent over and stretched back up and did not fall. I shouted, "Praise Yeshua my healer! I'm back to life! Halleluyah!" I took a good shower and dressed in a nice outfit. I went and sat down in the couch in my living room. My heart was full of gratitude toward Yehovah my God for giving us Yeshua! I looked back to what I had lived through over that weekend and realized that I could have died. But I was still alive and regaining my strength. I took that piece of paper and destroyed it. I felt hungry. I drank a cup of fruit juice. It was the first food that I had in three (3) days.

Then, I remembered that I had promised to cook a Sunday dinner to a couple of friends I had recently met in Chicago. They discovered my cooking and liked it. I checked the time. It was one (1) hour away from the dinner. I had no provision for the occasion. The entire week, I was in training and over the weekend Satan had fought me throughout. No excuse since I'm still alive! I rushed to the nearest grocery store and bought some grilled chicken, frozen french cut potatoes, and ketchup. I rushed back and threw the chicken and frozen potatoes in the oven. I had lost my taste and couldn't trust my seasoning. I knew I would have to wait and see the reactions of my guests. They were not that pleased. It was not the home meal that they were expecting. I apologized and told them I had a bad weekend and that I will fix it! Praise God! I'm alive and still going strong in Yeshua! Halleluyah! That bad Adversary had lost again!

C

Las Vegas Versus Yeshua

This event took place in the south side of Chicago, early 2001. It was the first sharing of the Good News with instantaneous result, after I had yielded to the call of Yeshua to preach the Good News of the Kingdom of Yehovah again in America. I used to do it before leaving Benin. However, in the US, I was focused on getting my graduate studies started while working to make a living. It is worth mentioning that when I finally yielded to the calling, I prayed that Holy Spirit takes the few words I will speak and do whatever He wants with them. It was a Friday. The first results of that prayer came within three (3) days. Holy Spirit turned me from being just "an encouraging brother" in Yeshua (Jesus, back then) to an engaging one. Until then, I used to encourage some so-called Christians in my newly built relationships, to take seriously their relationship with Yeshua. To this end, that same Friday, I called a young lady and promised to take her to a church on the following Sunday, so she could recommit her life to Yeshua.

That Sunday, while I was on my way to her house, I called her. She said that she was at work and would not be able to go to church as agreed. I asked the reasons for that sudden change. "My boss called me to come to work," she responded. She is a hairdresser. "Where is your boss now?", I asked. "She is here at work," she replied. I asked her for the address. She gave it to me. I said, "We are going to have church at your workplace!" She said "Nooo! Brother Luc"! I said "Yep! I'm already coming!" Once on the site, I asked to see the boss. She came to meet me in the hall of the store. I respectfully introduced myself and explained the reason why I had come. A bit puzzled, the boss pointed at the "bait lady" (to be clarified soon) and said, "She is working". With a smile I replied, "In that case, let's have church here, right now. I have my Bible!" On hearing this, some curious workers turned to listen more of this awkward conversation.

The boss then invited me in her office, closed the door, and bent her head over her desk for a moment. I was seating silently. I do not remember even praying in my heart. Then she raised her head to speak. I noticed that both of her eyes were red to tears. I kept silent while looking at her. She said, "My life is a mess! I just came from Vegas emptier than before going. I went to have fun, hoping to find a meaning to my life. On the contrary, I am more devastated! I have a serious emptiness inside that I cannot fill". At that point I told her that I understood the emptiness she was talking about. I also told her that I knew how to fill it. I told her that everyone who does not have Yeshua in their life, has more or less of that emptiness. All personal efforts, regardless of race, location, riches, or poverty fall short of filling permanently that emptiness. I told her that the emptiness is entertained by the Adversary of Yehovah God who created all humans and wants us to live a good and fulfilling life. I added that the Adversary of God is also her adversary. He works through her mind, emotions, and body to push her down and steal her joy.

How *He* Got Me Started

As I was talking, her face was filled with tears. I told her that amid this chaos, there is the Good News that shoot down from heaven. That Good News is that Yeshua, the Son of God came, took our side, fought, and defeated that very mean Adversary, Satan, about two thousand (2000) years ago. At this, her eyes cleared up. I told her that since then, Yeshua has been filling that emptiness in millions of hearts around the globe. He has been filling that big hole inside anyone who wants to let Him come into his or her life. I told her that right there, in her office at that very moment Yeshua could take care of her and fill her up, if she was ready to let Him come into her heart. "I am ready!" She replied. Then I opened my Bible and read to her Mark chapter 16 verses 14-19. I told her that by not living according to the Instructions of Yehovah, all human race and creation have brought a curse on themselves; curse that the Adversary has been enforcing and will continue to enforce until Yeshua returns.

I repeated to her that the Good News is that if she confesses her disobedience (things that she did wrong), renounces them with the resolve to remain obedient to God, accepts Yeshua as the Only Son of God and the only Way to Him, and gets immersed in water, she will be saved, because Yeshua will come into her life. The Adversary will no longer have a claim against her. Then, she said again, "I am ready to accept Jesus as my Savior, right now! I also want to be immersed in water." Then, I said, "Praise God! stand up, please!"

As I started praying thanking and praising Yehovah, she burst into abundant crying and gradually went flat on the floor of her office. I helped her back on her knees. She prayed and declared Yeshua as her Savior and the only Son of Yehovah God. I helped her get back up on her feet. I asked her how she was feeling afterward. "Very glad!" She responded. "The emptiness is gone!" She exclaimed! Joyfully we hugged amid laughter and praising Yehovah our God for the miracle!

We made arrangements for her to be immersed as soon as possible. Now a question for you: "That day, didn't we have church in that office?" Yes! Of course! We did! Praise Yehovah our God Almighty and Yeshuah His Holy Lamb forever! When we came out of the office, the "bait lady" was speechless. "What was that? And my boss is so joyful and unrecognizable", she must have asked herself. I told her that I will call her when she finishes her workday. The boss (nicknamed Lucky) accompanied me to my car. She then surprised me with something I could never had anticipated. She handed to me a piece of paper with a name and telephone number on it. She said, "Please, call this man. He is in a very dangerous mental state. Right now, he is full of rage. He recently bought a gun and is ready to kill." I took the piece of paper and said goodbye. What happened next is beyond imagination.

How *He* Got Me Started

[18] *Then Yeshua came and spoke to his disciples, "All power and authority have been given to me in Heaven and in Earth.* [19] *Go! ...* [20] *Teach all nations to carry out all the things I have commanded you – forever."*

Matt 28v18-20

D

Prayed Over The Phone And Holy Spirit "Beat Up" A Brother

This event is the follow-up of the previous one about how Lucky, the owner of the hairdressing business, accepted Yeshua as her Savior. Once I returned to my apartment in the north side Chicago that Sunday afternoon, I prayed and thanked God and Yeshua for a great day. I was full of joy and gratitude about how Yeshua made me "catch my first fish" in America for His Kingdom. Then I remembered the piece of paper. I pulled it out of the pocket of my jacket. I took a good look at it and placed it on the coffee table in my living room. Then I engaged a conversation with Holy Spirit in these terms: "A gun! On the first day in the field of ministry! Welcome to America! Is it really what you have for me? I'm not so sure about the gun part. I have already heard enough about gun issues in Chicago. Especially in the South Side." So, I went about my business with no clear idea on what to do with the piece of paper.

The following Tuesday night Holy Spirit told me to fast and pray about the piece of paper. So, I did for three (3) days - Wednesday to Friday and closed. Around 7:00 pm I picked up the famous piece of paper and called the number. A deep male voice answered at the other end of the line. I said, are you Bernard? He said "Yes! What do you want?" I told him that someone gave me the number to call and see how he was doing. "I'm alright!", he said in a hostile tone of voice. I said, "That is all. But if you don't mind, I could pray for you". "Pray for what?", he said. Still with the same hostile tone of voice. I said, "A quick prayer, if you don't mind." He said, "Go ahead!" So, I prayed saying:

> *Thank you God for the life of Bernard. You have created him, and you love him. I commit his life into your hand. I don't know what he is going through. But you do. In the mighty name of Yeshua, I pray that you change his situation to better. Amen!*

I heard no reaction. Then I said, "Goodbye!" With the same hostile tone of voice, he replied, "Bye"! And that was it. I hung up the phone and moved on with my evening.

Around 10:00 pm, I got a surprise phone call. It was Bernard on the other end of the line. He said, "Are you the one who called me earlier?" I said, "To pray with you?" "Yes!", he replied. His tone of voice was better. I told him that I was the one who called to pray with him. "Were you in my apartment?" he asked. "No!" I replied. Then he said:

> *I just came back from work and sat down in my couch when you called. There was nobody else in the apartment beside me. However, after you prayed and hung up, while I was*

How *He* Got Me Started

still seating in the couch, something hit me hard from behind. Surprised, I angrily turned to see what that was. Then I got like a slap from behind. And another slap, and another one. I fell from the couch to the floor. The beating continued while I was rolling on the floor trying to block whatever was slapping me. I was trying to see. But I could not see what was slapping me. It was very hard on me. Then I heard a voice that said, 'why did you buy the gun? Who do you want to kill?' At that point, I fainted. About two (2) hours later I regained consciousness. I got up, took the gun, and went into the streets in search for the nearest gutter opening. I found one and threw the gun in. I just returned home and decided to call you.

I said, "Bernard! God loves you and does not want you to ruin your life by killing anyone with that gun. What happened to you is a correction from God. Just as a loving father does correct his child, God sent his Spirit, Holy Spirit to correct you. I was not in your apartment. Not at all! I had no consciousness of being in your apartment, although with God, ALL things are possible. You need to know that there is an Adversary of God, called Satan who pushes the children of God to destroy their own lives, or destroys those lives himself. However, because Yehovah God loves you and me and the whole humanity so much, He did do something big about two (2) thousand years ago. He sent Yeshua His ONLY Son to fight Satan for us.

The Good News is that Yeshua successfully defeated the Adversary! Now if you believe it, the Peace of God that you could not have ever imagined will fill your heart and you will become a better person that you could not have ever imagined. Do you believe it? He said, "I believe it". Then I read to him what Yeshua said in Mark chapter 16 verses 14-19 and pointed out to him that the belief he now has MUST be followed by his immersion in water without delay. After some explanation, I asked him if he was ready to get immersed into water. He replied, "Yes! I'm ready". I made with him the same arrangements I made with Lucky for the same following Sunday morning.

On that Sunday morning, to my great surprise, when I got to our appointment, Bernard was thirty (30) minutes ahead of time and waiting. Praise Yehovah our God! My second gun-related encounter in the field of ministry was in the North Side Chicago in 2003. It was a Los Angeles "repenting" gangster who found shelter in Chicago. One Sunday, while I was alone after service in OCC's building, he walked by the building. Once our eyes crossed, he stopped and asked to come in. I welcomed him and made him feel comfortable. Just as in the case of Bernard, I did not see the gun and the gun did not come near me. But Holy Spirit "arrested" him right there. Praise God! He introduced himself to me as LA. Later before his immersion in water, he told me that his real name was Larome. Shalom, brother Larome, if you are reading this testimony! I thank Yehovah for your new life in Yeshua. There was no dramatic dealing of Holy Spirit with him that I was made aware of. However, after a couple of one-on-one meetings, he decided to abandon his old life and accept Yeshua as the Savior. We celebrated and immersed him in water. He was also taken through deliverance, a prayer process of sanctification and breaking of strongholds of the Adversary in the lives of believers in Yeshua. Praise be to Yehovah God for His love for Bernard, Lucky, Larome, and for the whole world! I remain assured that this reading will always stir them up wherever they may be. I desire to see them again on this earth. If not, then see you in Heaven with Yeshua our Savior and friend.

How *He* Got Me Started

⁴⁷ *and that repentance and remission of sins should be preached in his name among all nations, beginning at Yerushalayim.* ⁴⁸ *You are witnesses of these things.* ⁴⁹ *Now, behold, I will send the promise of my Father upon you, but tarry in the city of Yerushalayim until you are endued with power from on high.*

Luke 24v47-49

E

Prayed For The Gift Of Visions But Was Anointed Prophet

As the news of the salvation of Lucky and Bernard was broadcast through their different networks of relationships, so was my name. As a result, more people had accepted Yeshua. We then created a group to meet for Bible study and prayer every Sunday afternoon. Among us was a sister named Priscilla. She was a very God-fearing lady. I respected and admired her a lot. I still do, although I have not been able to keep contact with her. She was endowed with the gift of visions. She used to close her eyes during our prayer meetings, see, and share with us, things that made our intercessory prayers very effective. I appreciated that gift so much that toward the end of year 2001, I asked Yeshua to give me that gift of visions as well.

Mid-year 2002, while sleeping at night, I saw myself in a vision and heard a voice of authority rebuke some evil spirits that were about to hurt me, by saying to them, "What are you doing there? Don't you know that he is my Prophet!" It was at that moment that I knew that Yeshua has anointed me his Prophet and had just thrown it in the face of the Adversary as a warning. Praise be to Yehovah our God and to Yeshua His Holy Lamb our Deliverer. What happened afterwards was beyond interesting.

F

Proclaimed Prophet In Three Instances Over Two Continents

First Time

I will be referring to the vision in which I heard the voice of authority referring to me as "His Prophet" against some evil spirits. Once the vision was over, I woke up suddenly. I then kneeled by my bed side and prayed saying:

> *Thank you, my God, for the vision and for calling me your Prophet. I accept it. However, I have a request: I know that in America, Prophets are not welcome. Same thing I have noticed while in Africa. Prophets are not accepted. Please, before I refer to myself as Prophet, make it first come out of the mouth of the people.*

My request was granted and manifested in three dramatic instances twice in America and once in Africa, until now. Praise Yehovah our God and Yeshua our Savior for their Goodness.

From that day, it was like a trail started after me in Chicago. Questions about who I was, that I did not get before that request, started to be thrown at me. It happened in conversations on the train, the bus, with individuals who already knew me or individuals whom I had met for the first time. The question was, "so, are you an Apostle, a Pastor, an Evangelist, or…?" To get away, I used to respond with a smile by saying, "If you see me driving a taxi, call me taxi driver. If you see me sharing the Good News, call me Evangelist or Preacher." I used to escape with that kind of answer until one day, there was no way of escape.

This time it was not on a train, a bus, or during a casual talk. It was during a bible study meeting of elders and leaders in a church in Evanston, Illinois. A lady who was an elder, abruptly stopped the meeting when she raised her voice and pointed her finger at me saying, "So, brother Luc! Are you a Prophet?" Taken by surprise, everyone was looking at her including myself, while she was gazing at me with her finger still pointing. I did not answer. The room went silent for about half a minute or so. I still did not answer her. The Pastor broke the silence by saying, "Brother Luc! Please, answer the question!" Then, my mouth opened, and I said, "Yes! I am!" The lady, a bit heavy in stature, grabbed the meeting table and shook it while screaming, "I knew it! I knew it! I knew it!" We all broke into praising Yehovah for some time.

When things settled, I asked to speak. I shared the vision with them including my request that just got fulfilled for the very first time, before their eyes. That took us on another round of praise. They hugged me, prayed for me, and started calling me Prophet Luc until the day I left their congregation years later. Sister Anderson is the lady and Thomas Glasford is the Pastor. Praise Yehovah! I thought, that was it, after that day! But no! It was just the first round with the saints of Yehovah.

Wait for the second round! It happened a few months later in a grocery store in the North Side Chicago. It was a Sunday early afternoon.

¹³ *When Yeshua came into the coasts of Caesarea Philippi he asked his disciples, "Who do men say that I, the Son of Man, am?"* ¹⁴ *They replied, ... "some say that you are Eliyahu, and others say you are Yirmeyahu or one of the prophets." ...* ¹⁶ *Shimon Kefa answered, "You are the Messiah, the Son of the living Elohim."* ¹⁷ *Yeshua said to him, "Blessed are you, Shimon ben Yonah, for flesh and blood have not revealed it to you, but my Father in heaven.*

Matt. 16v13-17

How *He* Got Me Started

Second Time

We returned from a convention and Pastor Thomas dropped me at a grocery store to pick up some groceries. We were away from town for a couple of days because of a convention. As I entered the first alley in the store, I got stopped right behind a lady who was picking up some produce on the shelf. She had her back turned at me. I could not see her face. I was surprised to realize that I was staring at the back of her head. Sometimes when someone is intensely looking at you from your back or the side, you can feel it. It could be what happened to her. She felt it.

So, she turned her face to see me. Right at that moment I pointed my finger toward her face and in a tone of voice of authority I said, "I know you, woman!" To my amazement, she screamed with fear in her eyes and face, "You are the Prophet! You are the Prophet"! She dropped her shopping basket with all the produce on the floor at my feet and ran out of the grocery store. I was still standing. She slammed the door of the store and disappeared from my view. That was it!

Inside the store, as some shoppers who were surprised by the scene started looking at me with questioning eyes, I sped up through the alleys to mind my business. That was the second time! To Yehovah our God be All the glory from generation to generation and forevermore.

³¹ *Yeshua came down to Kfar Nahum, a village of the lower Galilee, and he taught them on Shabbat days.* ³² *They were astonished at his doctrine, and his speech was with authority.* ³³ *In the synagogue there was a man who had a spirit of an unclean demon, and he cried out with a loud voice,* ³⁴ *"Leave us alone! What have we to do with you, Yeshua of Natzeret? Have you come to destroy us? I know who you are! The Holy One of* יהוה*.*

Luke 4v31-34

How *He* Got Me Started

Third Time

Years went by. I did not know that Yeshua had a third round in waiting. This time in Africa, in year 2022 in Benin, twenty (20) years after the second round in Chicago, USA. That year, I was on a trip to Benin. I was informed by a relation that a Pastor of the United Methodist Church of Côte d'Ivoire was on a short trip to Benin for his Ph.D. research work and will need a place to stay. He knew nothing about me relative to ministry, except that I was a brother in Christ. I prepared his accommodations and he arrived. The following morning after his first night, I went to check on him, because he arrived on a very late-night flight. To my surprise, he was already dressed up and about to go to church. It was a Sunday. I heard him coming down and I decided to wait for him downstairs. As soon as he saw me, he exclaimed, "Hello, Mr. Luc! Are you a Bishop?" With a smile I asked him why he said it. He replied that the way I was standing, and the office-like door next to me, made him say it. We had a quick chat and he left for his business.

On the third day, in the evening, I went to check on him. He asked me if I set up a camera in his room. I said, "No! Why?" He said that a couple of times he thought about reorganizing the furniture in a particular way and when he returned, he checked and was told that I came around and did do the change he wanted without him telling me. Then he added, "beyond a camera, what about my own thoughts? Things I did not voice out to anyone. Not even to my driver. Things I forgot to do or buy. When I get back to the residence, I find that they have been taken care of or made available to me. Now you scare me, brother Luc! Are you a Prophet?". Through a laughter, I escaped the question. I thought because he is a man of the Spirit he would know.

On the seventh day he told me that he planned to travel to Lome the capital city of the neighboring country Togo. About two hours and a half drive. "With which car?" I asked him. He replied that he will be riding in the same rental car he has been using since his arrival. I told him that the car will break down on the way and he will not like it. Instead, I offered him to take the car available in this residence. It is a 4x4 vehicle in great shape. He declined and said that he is confident that everything will be alright with his car. I did not insist. The following day, very early in the morning, I showed up to wish him a safe journey and prayed that they have a nice trip. He was supposed to return the same day by sundown.

To my surprise, after 9:30 pm he had still not returned. I could not reach neither him nor his driver over the phone. I prayed that all is well with them. Close to 11:00 pm he called me and said that the car broke down badly and they could not get any effective help to fix it. He added that for more than three hours he had been experiencing misery after misery until a few minutes ago when finally, they walked into the lobby of a descent hotel. I shared some encouraging words with him and prayed that the night brings them comfort.

The following day, by the grace of Yehovah, they fixed the car and were able to drive back safely to Benin. In the evening, I went to check on him at his residence. When he saw me, he exclaimed, "You are a Prophet! You are a Prophet! You are a Prophet! My God! Everything you told me was true!" I replied, "To the glory of Yehovah our God and of Yeshua His Holy Lamb and our Savior". He went on to share the details of his misery on the return trip from Lome, Togo. The next day, an assistant at the residence told me that the Pastor said that I was a Prophet. I asked him why he said it. He replied that Pastor said that everything I told him was true. This is how Yeshua made the third proclamation! Praise His holy

How *He* Got Me Started

name forever! Interestingly enough, this time He chose to do it in Benin by the mouth of one of His servant Pastor Affi from Côte d'Ivoire while on a trip in Benin. My wife had known Pastor Affi for years, although they had no ongoing relationship. Our children had the opportunity to meet him for the first time during that trip. Praise be to Yehovah our God from generation to generation and forevermore!

G

Slapped A Demon And It Sounded Like A Thousand Thunders

This event happened in the same vision of 2002 in Chicago when I was called Prophet. During my sleep, I was caught up in a vision and saw myself sleeping in what looked like a floating bed in the sky. All around my body was foggy white. I could not see anything else. Suddenly, appeared some dark clouds having different shapes. As I was watching, they surrounded my body. I understood that these were evil spirits ready to hurt me. Right at that moment, a voice of authority spoke saying, "what are you doing there? Don't you know that he is my Prophet?" Automatically, the evil spirits retreated away from my body which was still laying on the bed with my cover on. I noticed that one of the dark clouds returned and was pulling out a shape that looked like a foot. I understood that this particular evil spirit was about to kick me.

In a flashing move, I rose from under my cover and slapped that demon so hard, it sounded like a thousand thunders! It was so loud that it pulled me violently from my sleep. I leaped out of the bed wondering what kind of thunderstorm was out there. It was much louder than anything I had ever heard in my life. I rushed to the window and swung the curtain to look. I was residing on the 8th floor of the building. To my biggest surprise, the sky was very calm and quiet. The stars were shining in a very beautiful sky. There was no rain! No lighting or storm!

While I was still under shock and confused, I heard the voice of Holy Spirit speak inside of me saying, "You just had a vision". I turned and dropped on the floor by my bed and prayed, saying, "I thank you Father God! I thank you Yeshua my Savior! I thank you Holy Spirit my comforting Counselor! I thank you for calling me your Prophet. I accept it. I thank you for showing me that you are protecting me from evil spirits." Then I made the request that you have previously read. In all and above all, I give praise and glory to Yehovah our God who seats on His Holy Place and rules in the affairs of mankind here on earth. Halleluyah!

How *He* Got Me Started

²³ *There was in their synagogue a man with an unclean spirit who cried out...* ²⁵ *Yeshua rebuked him, "Silence! Come out of him!"* ²⁶ *When the unclean spirit had trashed him and cried with a loud voice, he came out of him.*

Mark 1v23-26

H

Chased A Demon-Possessed Out Of A Church

This took place in the North Side Chicago in 2003, inside the building where the former gangster Larome accepted Yeshua as His Savior. Under the direction of Holy Spirit, I went on a fasting from Wednesday to Saturday to spend time in the presence of Yehovah. I had no specific request; just wanting to spend time in fasting and prayer! After I closed the fasting and prayer on that Saturday evening, I decided to take a shower. On my way to the bathroom, I overheard a mocking voice that addressed me saying, "Ha! You fasted! Did you get anything out of it?" Indeed, throughout the fasting and prayer, there was no spiritual or physical manifestation. There was no message. There was nothing that I could say that I received from that 3-day consecration. However, inside of me, was that confidence that things that I could not see in the spiritual realm had happened for my benefits. So, I answered back the Adversary in these words, "Really! Well! You will see what I have gotten!" Then I took my shower and enjoyed my Saturday night relaxed.

On Sunday morning, I decided to meet pastor Shawn C. Woodie of Outreach Community Church (OCC) at their North Side Chicago branch. I had previously requested his permission to use their church building for meetings. However, for some reason, the approval process was being delayed. It is worth noting that I am not a member of OCC. The church service was already going when I arrived. I used the back door to enter and sat among the congregants in the middle section. I bent my head in prayer with my eyes closed for a few minutes. Then I heard an awkward noise toward the back, followed by the noise of chairs being pushed around violently and some hard human breathing. I raised my head with my eyes open to see and understand what was happening. To my surprise, all the congregants had their faces turned toward the back of the building with scary expressions. Some attendants were standing. Nevertheless, Pastor Woodie was still standing on the pulpit preaching. I thought they were looking at me. But no! Something scary was going on behind me. I turned to look. Oh! What a scene! A demon-possessed lady with seriously scary eyes and face was sending the ushers flying. Whenever they tried to grab and take control of her, in a couple of movements of her arms, she pushed the ushers so violently that they landed among the chairs and on congregants who were nearby.

The power of Holy Spirit arose in me. I grabbed my Bible and walked toward her. An usher tried to stop me. I ignored him and advanced with my eyes focused on the demon-possessed lady. She was still fighting the ushers. She did not see me coming until I was about five (5) feet from her. I raised up the Bible toward her face and in a voice of authority I said, "I come against you in the name of Yeshua and with the Word of God!" Surprisingly, the same usher said to me, "keep your voice down!

How *He* Got Me Started

The pastor is preaching". This time I turned to him and said, "In that case, go get her!" As expected, he withdrew to the side. I was not angry at him. He neither saw me nor knew me before. Then I turned to the demon-possessed lady and repeated, "I come against you in the name of Yeshua and with the Word of God"! I got her attention! Instantly, she stopped fighting the ushers but faced me with a threatening attitude. With the Bible raised up toward her face I repeated, "I come against you in the name of Yeshua and with the Word of God!" To the amazement of the whole attendance, she replied in a deep male voice unequal to that of a lady, "you cannot save me!" Her eyes were wide open and her face distorted. I said, "I do not want to save you. This is a sanctuary of God. Get out of here now!" She ran through the same back door I used to come in. The ushers closed it back and locked it.

Praise Yehovah! Order was restored and the service proceeded quietly. Praise Yehovah! Yeshua has indeed defeated Satan about two thousand years ago and gave us the power to walk in His Victory! Halleluyah! After the service, Pastor Woodie broke all the protocols and granted me access to the building and its key. Halleluyah! He put a deacon at my service to open and close the building whenever needed. A lady who was also a deacon, evangelist, and prayer warrior, member of OCC, volunteered herself to assist. I realized that the brother deacon was the one who was getting in my way. He was not an usher. I built a very strong relationship with these two deacons. Every time I had an event in Chicago even outside of OCC's building, they were with me to assist. The brother's name is Gregory Waheed and the sister's name is Lucil.

1

Prayed And Closed Another Psychic Business

This event took place in Blacksburg, Virginia in 2009. During one of my trips to pick up my wife from Virginia Tech campus where she was pursuing her Ph.D., I noticed an office of a psychic business near the campus. We were both surprised and unhappy to see such business in such place.

We stopped our car and prayed. We commanded the closure of that psychic business without delay. About two months later, on our return trip, we were happy and shocked by what we saw: not only had the psychic business closed, but there was a large and deep whole dug by an excavator. The place was turned into a new development site of the University. Halleluyah! We drove around to check if the psychic business had relocated anywhere else. But it was nowhere to be found!

J

Prayed And A Sound System Was Fixed Live

This event happened in 2003 in Illinois during a church convention. It was my first time attending this convention. I was with Pastor Thomas Glasford, other members and leaders. During the Sunday closing service, a Pastor of the church organization network was about to preach. In preparation for his message, the praise and worship team of his church took the stage to sing. The song should have started with a soundtrack play. I learned later that it was a big moment because of the fame of the praise and worship team. Unfortunately, the Adversary had sticked his hand into the track to ruin that moment of high expectations.

About two minutes into the play, the soundtrack started skipping. What embarrassment for the lead singer who tried hard to keep control of the situation and continue singing. About one minute into this awkwardness, Holy Spirit arose inside of me. I turned and saw the whole convention staring at the praise and worship team on the stage. I shouted at the congregation with a loud voice saying, "Pray! You have the power! Command that machine to work, now!" In response, the whole congregation burst into loud prayers. The Adversary was thrown out! The soundtrack stopped skipping! The praise and worship team unleashed their full power! The moment was saved! Halleluyah! Then, their pastor delivered his astonishing message.

    The next time I went to meet a brother at that church, they cheered me for having saved the face of the praise and worship team and that of their pastor. Praise be to Yehovah our God and to His Lamb who gave us power over the Adversary and demons. It was from this convention that Pastor Thomas dropped me in a store to grab a supply of groceries and a lady screamed "You are the Prophet" and ran through the door. Praise Yehovah!

How *He* Got Me Started

¹ *Yeshua called his twelve disciples and gave them power over unclean spirits, to cast them out, and to heal all manner of sickness and all manner of disease.*

Matt 10v1

K

Turned To Look At A Gay, And Two Of Them Ran Off

This event took place in the North Side Chicago in 2008 in the apartment of deacon Gregory Waheed from the OCC church. I mentioned him in the case of the demon-possessed lady whom I chased out of a church service. This brother invited me to attend his fiftieth birthday celebration. He was residing on the 18th floor of a high-rise near Lake Shore Drive. When I arrived, the living room of the apartment was already packed, and some guests were chatting in the hallway. The brother pulled me in and made me sit. I was surprised that there was still one empty seat on my right. Then two gentlemen squeezed into the living room. By their appearance, you could easily tell that they are gay. Due to the lack of seats, one of them returned and stood not far from the entrance door, while the other took the seat on my right side.

Immediately, he turned to me and said, "You are different!" I responded by nodding my head and kept my face straight while remaining silent. A few minutes later, he turned to me again and said, "You are not like others. You are different." This time I did not respond. The next moment, the deacon stepped forward and said to me while pointing his finger at the guy in my right, "Brother Luc! Pray for this guy!".

When I turned to finally look at the guy, something happened that I could not have anticipated. He jumped from his seat and ran toward the exit door. His friend was doing the same thing. However, because the room was crowded and the door was jammed, he made a dangerous and deadly move. He took a leap toward the glass window of the 18th floor. Thankfully, the guests seating by that window grabbed him and hauled him down. The friend having forced his way through the door, the exit was finally possible. I calmly said, "Please, let him go!" Once released, he rushed through the door! All this happened in a flash, while I was still seating on my chair. What a moment! I prayed for the event, blessed the food, then left. To Yehovah our God and His Son Yeshua be all the glory from generation to generation and forevermore!

How *He* Got Me Started

¹⁴ *More and more believers were added to the Messiah, multitudes of both men and women.* ¹⁵ *They even brought the sick out into the streets on their beds and couches so that, at least, the shadow of Kefa passing by might fall upon some of them.*

                                                             Acts 5v14-15

L

Prayed For A Man And The Wife Almost Called The Police

This happened in 2014. I had moved to Northern Virginia with my family. The brother I prayed for was living in Lexington, Kentucky. After this event he moved his family to Texas. This brother was going through continued and serious attacks of the Adversary over his career and family for years until he heard about me. Then both of our families met in Kentucky during summer 2013. I prayed for them and returned to Virginia. Early winter of that year, however, he reported that the Adversary had been attacking him again. I prayed over the phone without success. Then we agreed that I should go to them, because he would not be able to bring his whole family for a prayer meeting in Virginia. My wife and I decided that she will stay while I go alone because her pregnancy started to weigh on her. I did not want to drive but fly, because of the winter snow. However, early January 2014, flights were being canceled all over our region due to heavy and dangerous snowfall.

As a result, I was locked down and could not fly. However, the situation of this brother and his family was getting worse by the week.

Mid-January, one night, I was still awake taking care of a few things until around 2:00 after mid-night. The thought of the brother came to my mind. An anger filled me against the Adversary for the pain he was inflicting him and his family, while the weather was preventing me from traveling. Thus, Holy Spirit arose inside of me. Although I had decided not to pray for him anymore over the phone, I grabbed the phone and called his number. I was happily surprised to hear him answer the call. I asked him if he was ready to pray at the moment. He said, "Yes!" I poured out all my anger through that line over the Adversary.

During the prayer, I could clearly hear him respond "Amen!" Nevertheless, after some time, I could no longer hear his response, although he did not hang up his phone. Then I heard an "Amen!" followed by a long deep breathing, and a silence. I continued the raging prayer for about forty-five minutes. Then I heard the voice of his wife over the phone, saying, "Amen! Prophet Luc!" I was surprised, because early in the prayer, her husband told me that she was sleeping with the kids upstairs, and that he would rather go downstairs in the living room for the prayer. Past that flash surprise, the prayer continued for an additional fifteen minutes or so until I stopped. Then, I said. "Hello! Hello!" But no one answered. I hung up, knowing that for sure, the husband was already knocked out! I prayed and thanked Yeshua for what He had done that I will hear about.

A few minutes later, his wife called me and said, "Prophet Luc! I did not know that my husband was praying with you. I was about to call 911." I said, "Really! Why"? She replied:

I was suddenly awakened by some disturbing noise. I looked

How *He* Got Me Started

and my husband was not in bed. I listened and it was not just noise, but scary screaming coming from downstairs. I covered myself better and decided to go check. As I was going down the stairs I recognized the voice of my husband. I was very disturbed. I wondered what was happening to him. For fear that he might jump on me or hurt me, I dialed 911 on my phone and had my thumb ready to press if anything goes wrong.

I said, "Really! Was it that scary?" "Yes!" she replied. She continued by saying:

When I got downstairs, the screaming and noise were coming from the guest toilet room. The door was opened. I looked and saw my husband on the floor. The look in his eyes and his face are nothing I had ever seen on him before. It was very scary! He was holding the plumbing pipes of the sink and not letting go! His phone was on the floor. Then I heard your voice over the phone. So, I managed to pick it up and said 'Amen' and pushed back the phone on the floor toward him and join you in prayer. Halleluyah! My husband is delivered! We are set free! I knew we were under attacks. Nevertheless, I could not have ever imagined that the Adversary had managed to possess parts of my husband's life this way! Thank you so much Yeshua my Savior! Thank you, Prophet Luc! Thank you very much! You will have to come and see some of the things that happened here!

I said "OK! We shall do, by the grace of Yehovah. But where is your husband now?" "Laying on the floor in the living room. He has not yet been talking," she replied. I said, "that is OK!" I prayed for her and hung up the phone.

The prayer of that night broke the back of the Adversary and removed the chains off their lives. After that major breakthrough, the brother and his wife could clearly see where the path of their destiny is leading them. As results, the husband changed job and the family moved to Texas. We had the blessed opportunity to meet again before their move. Among other details the husband later shared, is the fact that at a moment during the prayer, he started losing control of himself to the extent that he could no longer hold the phone in his hand. So, he let it fall. However, there was a power coming from my voice that was pulling some forces out of him. He felt good about it and did not want to be drawn away from the phone. Therefore, he decided to find an anchor. That is the reason why he grabbed hold of the plumbing pipe in the guest toilet where his wife found him. Praise Yeshua who set us free from the bondage of the Adversary and gave us power to kick him out of our lives! The couple's name are Mr. V. and Mrs. E. V.

How *He* Got Me Started

10 Yeshua was teaching in one of the synagogues on the Shabbat. 11 And, behold, there was a woman who had a spirit of infirmity for eighteen years, who was bent over, and could in no wise stand up. 12 When Yeshua saw her, he called her to him, and said to her, "Woman, you are loosed from your infirmity." 13 He laid his hands on her: and immediately she was made straight, and she glorified יְהֹוָה.

Luke 13v10-13

M

Immersed in Water and Could No Longer Speak And Eat

This event took place in Jumonville Retreat and Camp Center in Hopwood, Pennsylvania over the Labor Day weekend of September 2-5, 2011. The previous months, a brother from New York recommended a lady, friend of his, to contact me to hear the True Good News of God. At the time, I used to also hold nationwide bible studies and prayers over the phone. The lady was a generational devoted Catholic. She used to "enjoy life" with her friends. She could care less about any spiritual things but Catholicism. She later confessed that the only reason she contacted me was to clear her conscience and shut down her New York "bothering friend". However, to her surprise, she kept on coming. I remembered telling her that she will not regret it.

One day, she called me and said that she saw Yeshua in her dream, and she wants to accept Yeshua as her Savior. I rejoiced with her, read Mark 16 verses 15-18 to her. Then I told her that the next step will be the immersion in water, and asked her if she was ready. "Yes!" she replied. At that time, our Jumonville retreat was drawing near. So, we agreed that she will get immersed at the retreat. I had never met her until the day of the retreat. On site, everyone was excited to be at the retreat. Nevertheless, the new believer sister outdid them all. She was singing, dancing, hugging everyone. She was eating and drinking joyfully. It was remarkably good. In the evening of the first day (Friday), she was immersed in the swimming pool. I purposely did not lay hands on her to receive Holy Spirit. During my preparation time, I had asked Holy Spirit to freely visit us without the need for me to lay hands individually on participants.

Later in the night, we had a campfire meeting and prayed under the open sky, after which we had a time of testimonies. The sister testified that she had a terrifying moment during the prayer time. She continued to say that in the middle of the prayer, she felt something like a powerful force that came over her from above. She felt like the force was pulling her up. To resist, she pushed her feet in the ground. Therefore, she could not walk away from her position to find safety. She could not speak either. So, she stretched her hand toward the nearest person. Unfortunately, that sister did not realize that she was trying to communicate with her. At this, "I lost all hope!" she said, because the powerful force was still over her. Thankfully, the prayer ended not too long after that encounter. She was still under the shock. I told her that it was Holy Spirit immersing her. The whole attendance broke into celebrations. Then I prayed and asked Holy Spirit to immerse her again for all eyes to see.

The next morning, she came to the meeting room completely transformed in her person. She was totally different than the person she was the previous day when she arrived at the retreat center. The very first noticeable change was that she was short of words. Next thing, she became

How *He* Got Me Started

very calm and quiet. Then she lost her appetite for any kind of foods and drinks except for the little bit of water she drank. The radical change was obvious to everyone throughout Saturday and Sunday until we closed the retreat. After the end of the closing service, most of the brothers and sisters had gone outside to take goodbye pictures and pack. However, this especially blessed sister was still on her seat in the meeting hall with a couple of sisters including my wife, who were having individual private prayer time.

When I returned to the hall, I saw her laying flat on the floor. I anointed her with oil and prayed over her. Later, my wife told me that my prayer was answered because they saw Holy Spirit come over her again. I exclaimed, "Praise Yehovah! But how?" My wife explained that the sister was still on her seat very quiet, while she (my wife) was playing the piano. Then they realized that the sister started to shake. Her mouth and all her body were shaking. At this, my wife told her to open her mouth and praise God. As soon as the sister opened her mouth to utter a word, she fell to the floor. Other sisters who were around helped her stretch flat where I came to see her. Praise Yehovah! who answered our prayer and sent Holy Spirit to immerse her right after her immersion in water. She left the retreat completely transformed, inside out! Truly born again! She was a brand-new person since that night at the retreat. Halleluyah!

After the closing, she requested that some of us accompany her to pray in her house before she returns, because she had altars of catholic idolatry set up in her bedroom. We granted her request and sent a group of three sisters and me to her house for a fresh deliverance and cleansing prayer the same Sunday night; the day we closed the retreat. Of all the many items that were removed from her home and destroyed, there was this large and heavy Nativity scene board. It was naive in its appearance, but very deceitful. Its destruction was not an easy task either; especially the central multi-dimensional piece. Its resistance increased our rage to break it. What a surprise, once we broke it open! There was a miniature head of a bull inside the Nativity scene. This was not the visible bull that is expected to be in the main Nativity scene; but a bullhead engraved within the scene and not visible from the outside. It was just the head with its two horns painted black about one third of their length from the top down. Although very hard, we successfully demolished it. "It was not a cheap purchase!" the sister said.

Since then, her life and home were so cleansed that one of her very good old friends who visited her in the weeks following her two immersions, almost ran outside of her house, saying, "she is completely different and unrecognizable. Thus, she is no more coming to her house". The sister said that her old friend was so offended that she did not want to talk to her anymore. Instead, she complained to the catholic priest of her former parish. The priest wrote her a letter, demanding explanations for all the complaints that were reported to him, by many of her friends; a letter to which she never replied. In all, praise be to Yehovah our God and to Yeshua our Savior who gave us Holy Spirit and power over the powers of darkness. The sister's name is Laetitia and the organization under which we held the retreat was IDAEM.

How *He* Got Me Started

¹ *While Apollos was at Corinth, Shaul, having passed through the upper coasts, came back to Ephesus, and finding certain disciples,* ² *he said to them, "Have you received the Ruach Ha Kodesh since you believed?" And they said to him, "We have not even heard that there is such a thing as the Ruach Ha Kodesh." ...* ⁵ *When they heard this, they were immersed in the name of the Messiah Yeshua.* ⁶ *Shaul then laid hands upon them and the Ruach Ha Kodesh came on them and they spoke with tongues and prophesied.*

Acts 19v1-6

N

A Teaser Of Speaking In Tongues Spoke In Tongues

This event took place in the North Side Chicago in 2001. This sister got in touch with me as the echo of what Holy Spirit did for Bernard and Lucky spread around. She was dealing with a chronic headache that was becoming unbearable. After a couple of ministration and prayers, Yeshua healed her. Thus, she accepted Yeshua as her Savior. Her husband, after seeing the miraculous healing, accepted Yeshua as his Savior as well. With my team, we immersed them together in the Lake Michigan on the North Side shore in Chicago. We prayed over them to receive Holy Spirit with speaking in tongues. However, it did not happen immediately. Nevertheless, a few days later, one early morning, I received a phone call from the sister. Her tone of voice was full of excitement because she just spoke in tongues in her bedroom during her morning prayer. Halleluyah! Then she said, "But there is a problem!" "What problem?" I asked. "I do not want my husband to know about it." "Why?" I asked. She said, "My husband and I used to make fun of people who speak in tongues." We both burst into laughter! Then she added, "I was so embarrassed because my husband was in the next room, and I could not stop the speaking in tongues. So, I dug my head under my bed sheet until it stopped." Halleluyah! Praise Yehovah! The power of Holy Spirit is true and still working!

Not long after that blessing of speaking in tongues, the Adversary got mad and stole the husband's car that he drives to work. His wallet, driver's license, credit cards, computer, etc., were still inside the vehicle. They called me and we prayed. Without a car, commuting to work was very difficult for this new brother. So, they decided to buy a new car. However, they did not make me aware of their decision. Which is fine! However, one night I had a vision in my sleep. I saw the brother at a dealership walking around some cars. In the next scene, I saw him driving his car that was stolen. Then my eyes opened, and the vision ended. Holy Spirit explained to me that the couple was about to buy a new car, but the stolen car was recovered. Praise Yehovah and His Holy Lamb! The next morning, I called the sister and asked about her husband. She said, "He left home early for a dealership to buy a new car". I told her to call him right away and tell him NOT to buy a new car. For Holy Spirit had shown me that his stolen car was recovered. Looking back, it was a bold move on my part! You will soon understand why! So, she called her husband, and he did not buy the new car. However, the challenge was the waiting time and TRUSTING in the words that I gave them by Holy Spirit.

It is worth mentioning that this was my very first clear-cut vision regarding other people after I had asked to receive the gift of vision like that sister Priscilia, whom I mentioned in one of the accounts in this book. I did not ask Holy Spirit neither how long it will take before the car is recovered, nor how it will be recovered. Nevertheless, just a couple

How *He* Got Me Started

of days after they canceled the car buying transaction, the wife called me fully excited, saying, "We found our car! The stolen car!" "Halleluyah! But how?" I asked. She said:

> *The police just called my husband and told him that a car was found abandoned in the outskirt of the town with his information inside. He is to report to the police station for confirmation. So, he is on his way as we speak.*

We broke into praising Yehovah! It was a "win-win"! They got their car. I got my gift of visions! Halleluyah! A few hours later they both called me back with great joy! Indeed, it was their stolen car. Amazingly, everything was still inside the vehicle: computer, wallet, credit cards, cash, etc. Nothing missing. The vehicle suffered only a minor damage on the side. That was it! What an amazing God we serve! His name is Yehovah and Yeshua is His Holy Lamb who was sacrificed for our redemption! Halleluyah! Believe it now, before it is too late! The couple's name is Mr. and Mrs. John and Florence W.

O

Stretched Out His Hand And A Lady Was Lifted Off The Ground

This event happened in 2008, during a World Conference of Prophet Morris Cerullo in a hotel near O'Hare International Airport in Chicago. It was lunch break. Pastor Steve Munsey had just closed the morning session with one of his distinguished illustrated sermons. The atmosphere was Holy Spirit charged. Like other participants, I also left the main auditorium heading to my hotel room. In the main hallway, while I was walking, I noticed a lady who stepped a bit out of the flow of other walking participants, heading toward me. Once closed to me, she nodded her head in a greeting manner. I responded "Hi!" and stretched out my hand to shake her hand. At that moment, something happened that caught both of us by surprise; including the participants that were chatting nearby. As I stretched my hand, the lady was suddenly pushed backward with speed while trying to regain her balance.

I did not realize that it was my stretched hand that caused her to move backward. Instead, I tried to prevent her from falling by stretching my hand forward to grab her hands. But I just made the matter worse. Thankfully, some of the participants who were witnessing the scene, turned themselves into "catchers" and caught her. I still did not understand that my stretched hand was sending the lady "flying". I approached her and I raised my hand up intending to say, "I bless you"! At that moment something happened that made me finally understand that my stretched hand was causing the whole pushback. As soon as I raised my hand to bless her, she was lifted off the ground. I had to raise my head to see her face. Fear was in her eyes with her mouth opened in surprise of what was happening. She had no control over the interaction. So, I brought down my hand slowly. As my hand was coming down, so was the lady, until she stood again on her feet on the ground.

Finally, I understood that my hand stretched was moving the lady. Consequently, I blocked my two hands down on my lower body and said to her "God bless you!" and nodded my head. She responded "Amen!". I stood in place and did not move. I stood in place and made sure that she had walked away enough distance before I moved. "What was that?" I asked myself. "What just happened?" I continued pondering through the break.

Not long before the afternoon session resumed, we crossed paths again. This time, I knew what to do. I stopped and kept my hands down. She also stopped walking and kept a distance. Then she said to me, "continue the work of deliverance and repairing broken bridges". I responded, "Thank you! That is what I'm doing!" "You are welcome!" she replied and walked off, while I stood enough time for her to go. Praise Yehovah the God of mystery! I do not remember shaking anyone else hand for the rest of the day or experiencing that same manifestation ever again.

How *He* Got Me Started

¹¹ *By the hands of Shaul,* יְהֹוָה *worked special miracles,* ¹² *so that when handkerchiefs or clothes that had touched his body were brought to the sick, diseases left them, and evil spirit departed from them.*

Acts 19v11-12

P

Pointed His Finger And Decorative Angels Disappeared

This event took place in the city of Des Plaines, Illinois, about an hour from Chicago. It was in the house of a Christian lady whose church does not believe in healing in the name of Jesus Christ. They do not believe that speaking in tongues should continue to be preached and practiced, because it was prohibited by the Apostle Paul, according to her church doctrine. Same goes with casting out demons and the Adversary, because Jesus Christ killed all demons through His death on the cross, also according to the doctrine of her church. At the time, she was going through the trauma of multi-personality issues aggravated with severe migraine that were getting worse over the years. Pills, medical assistance, and prayers of her pastor were unable to heal her. But thank Yehovah our God for a sister friend of hers, sister Julie, from her church who connected us. She is originally from Syria and believes all that their church does not believe. I pray the doctrine of this church has changed by now, in the mighty and supreme name of Yeshua our Mashiach.

As a last step in the process of assisting that Christian lady, together with two other leaders of the ministry, we had a night of deliverance prayers in her home. Once we concluded the meeting, she accompanied us outside and stood at the entrance door of her house. When I turned to say goodbye, my eyes were set on two "decorative statues of angels", each on the vertical doorframe of her house entrance door. Moved by Holy Spirit, I raised my right hand toward them and said, "What are you doing there? This is your last night!". We all witnessed that moment and I added no other words. We got into the car and drove away.

The next day, in the morning, the sister from Syria, sister Julie, who did not attend the prayer the previous night, called me with great excitement saying, "Prophet Luc! Our God is mighty! The decorative angels you threatened last night disappeared! My friend told me that this morning!" We praised God together for a moment, then I asked her how it happened. She said that in that morning her sister called her with great amazement saying that when she returned home from grocery shopping, she noticed that the two "angels" were missing from her front door. She was shocked! Praise Yehovah our God and Yeshua His Holy Lamb and our Savior, from generation to generation and forevermore!

How *He* Got Me Started

²⁷ *When Yeshua departed from the home of Yair, two blind men followed him, crying, "Son of David, have mercy on us!"* ²⁸ *When he came to his house, the blind men came to him and Yeshua said to them, "Do you believe that I am able to do this?" They said to him, "Yes, master."* ²⁹ *Then he touched their eyes, saying, "According to your faith, be it unto you."* ³⁰ *Their eyes were opened...*

Mat. 9v27-30

Q

A "Sick And Blind" Donation Almost Killed A Brother

This event happened in Toledo, Ohio, early 2005. At the conclusion of a ministerial trip to Toledo, a brother volunteered to donate a car (an SUV) to the work of the ministry. The news brought good cheers among the brethren. I drove the car back to Chicago. However, I noticed that the vehicle was not in good shape. I brought this to the attention of the brother. I asked him if he gave the car to Prophet Luc as a person or to God. He argued about it. So, we read in Malachi chapter 1 how God reproached his servants who were making undignified donations. And how He said that He will "turn their blessings into curses" in chapter 2 verse 2. He insisted that the car was in great shape and dealership certified, although he did not have the certificate. By the end of the conversation, he got very angry. In conclusion, I said to him, "you will see it when I soon come back to Toledo for the next conference". The car stayed parked just as it was since its arrival in Chicago.

The following month, I drove the vehicle back safely to Toledo, Ohio; a drive slightly over four hours. At my destination, I called the brother. He came with a friend and took the car for examination. Approximately fifteen minutes later, my phone rang. It was the brother on the line. He screamed, "My God! My God! Prophet Luc! I almost died! I almost died!" I replied calmly but very concerned, "Thank Yehovah! You are alive! What happened?" He said that as he accelerated the car on the ramp to take the highway, the front driver side tire spun off from beneath the car, which hit the road very hard. "It was terrifying", he added. "I'm very grateful that I was neither on the highway nor hit by cars coming behind on the ramp. This car almost killed me! You were right, Prophet Luc! The car is no good!"

After carefully inquiring about their safety, I prayed for them. I also told him that I appreciate his willingness to donate the car to the work of the ministry. However, it is better that he does not bring it back. And that was the end! Regardless of this incident, I continue to love this Jewish brother dearly. His name is Cornelius! Through his connections I was invited to minister to the Full Gospel Business Men's Fellowship chapel in Toledo. During this meeting, I also immersed in the swimming pool of the hotel a Jewish sister. In all, praise Yehovah our God who watches over His Word to accomplish it! To Him be the glory from generation to generation and forevermore!

How *He* Got Me Started

³⁶ *At that time Yoseph (Yosef), who by the apostles was surnamed bar Nava (son of a prophet), a Levite from the island of Cyrus,* ³⁷ *sold land that he owned, and he brought the money and laid it at the apostles' feet.* ¹ *Then a certain man named Ananias, with Sapphira his wife, sold a possession* ² *and secretly kept back part of the price, his wife also being privy to it. He brought a portion of the proceeds and laid it at the apostles' feet.* ³ *But Kefa said, "Ananias, why has hasatan filled your heart to lie to the Ruach Ha Kodesh and to keep back part of the price of the land?* ⁴ *Before you sold it, was it not your own land?...You have not lied to men, but to* יְהוָה *."* ⁵ *When Ananias heard these words, he fell down dead...*

Acts 4v36-37 to Acts 5v1-5

R

Spoke In Tongues In His Sleep And Fell Twice From The Bed

This event took place in Toledo Ohio, in early 2005. I was sharing a hotel room with Pastor Thomas who was mentioned in some of the previous events. We were hosting a deliverance conference in a hotel in the outskirt of downtown Toledo. In the morning after the first or second night, Pastor Thomas started laughing and said, "Prophet Luc! Do you know what you did last night in your sleep?" Very surprised, I asked what I did. Still with laughter, he replied, "You were praying in tongues in your sleep and fell to the floor twice. It was so intense that you rolled and fell. Each time you fell, you crawled back into your bed and continued speaking in tongues". I said, "Really? Halleluyah! I really got it!" To be speaking in tongues in my sleep with a witness of the status of a pastor, to testify about it, made it undoubtedly true! Thank you, Holy Spirit, for putting your seal on it for me in this very special manner! Praise your Holy name! Oh! Yehovah my God!

S

Got Help Twice From Angels In International Airports

First Occurrence

This event happened twice. The first, in early December 2017 at Dulles International Airport (IAD) in Northern Virginia. The second, in early August 2019, two years later, at Newark Liberty International Airport, New Jersey. In the first case, on the way to an international trip, together with my wife and children, we booked a couple of days in a hotel near the airport to avoid the last minute rush. Early in the morning, on the day of the trip, we arrived at IAD from our hotel. It was a cloudy day with light rain. As soon as we got out of the taxi, we had our first nice surprise.

On the curb, a black man of high physical stature wearing a light dark raincoat approached us with a smile. He greeted us saying, "Hello people of [he said the name of our international destination], [greeted us in the language of our destination]." My wife and I responded warmly and told him the airline we were flying with. At that very moment my wife realized that I forgot a suitcase in the hotel. The man led me speedily to the taxi lane and got me into the very first one with instructions to rush me to my hotel to get my forgotten suitcase. Inside the taxi, I started wondering about these two acts of the man who welcomed us on the curb of the airport.

When I returned with the suitcase, I saw the man standing by my wife and children. They were still at the counter checking-in the last suitcase except for the one I just brought in. My wife told me that the man helped her with all the luggage and helped them get in line just on time before the airline closed the check-in. "We are the last passengers whose luggage are being processed." She added. I turned to the man. Thanked him and asked his name. "George!" he replied. I wanted to give him a tip (cash money). But he declined and said: "Let's get going. You are now running late because of the trip back to the hotel". I was happily surprised that he was still willing to continue helping us. He directed us toward immigrations (passport and visa check) and said, "I will meet you there". That was his act 4 after: 1) greeting us in our destination language with the mention of the destination without us telling him, 2) directing me diligently to a taxi, and 3) assisting my wife with the check-in of all our suitcases and declining the tip.

My wife and I started enjoying the company of Mr. George. It is worth mentioning that my wife was pregnant. While we were in line and getting closer to the immigration desk, Mr. George appeared on our side of the line. This time he had no raincoat on. He was wearing a uniform with SECURITY written on the back and front of his T-shirt. He told my

How *He* Got Me Started

wife to organize our passports. Then, he collected and submitted them to the immigration officer. He walked around and stood behind the officer. Once stamped, he collected all our passports and made a sign to us to follow him. His act 4 was completed. We were now heading to the TSA (Transportation Security Administration) scanners.

The line was extremely long. Mr. George instructed us to get out of the line and follow him on the sidelines. Whenever it became hard to move about, he would say, "Excuse me!". It happened a couple of times. In response, mostly, travelers showed resistance and frustration until they turned to see who was asking for the way. Once they saw standing behind them, a man of high physical stature in uniform with SECURITY written on his chest, they surrendered and made the way. However, they always gave us that look, which can be interpreted as "Who is this couple, who is this family for a security agent to be leading them?" Once he "accelerated" us to the scanner, he said, "I will see you on the other side". Which he did. His act 5 was completed.

He appeared again when we were boarding the train to our flight terminal to make sure we were on the right track. Nevertheless, we did not see him getting on the train. When we reached our flight boarding area, to our good surprise Mr. George was already there and standing by the flight attendants who also gave us a very warm welcome. After the long walk, of course my pregnant wife needed to use the lady's room before boarding the plane. And for that also, Mr. George directed her quickly. We said, "Thank you very much, Mr. George!" We greeted him goodbye and boarded the plane with great joy. It was amazing what we had just experienced.

At our final destination, my wife and I talked about Mr. George. We received that inner assurance that Mr. George was our angel sent from

Yehovah to assist us in the physical. Upon our return to the US, I had told my wife a couple of times that I would like us to drive to IAD airport to see angel George. However, inside of me a voice always said, "Since you know that he is an angel, why will you go there looking for him?" Thus, we never did, although we had flown through that airport multiple times since 2017, with more children with and without a pregnancy. What an amazing God we have! God of wonders! Halleluyah!

How *He* Got Me Started

¹ Now about that time King Herod began to persecute particular members of the kehilah. ² He killed Ya'akov, the bother of Yochanan, with the sword, ³ and because he saw it pleased the prushim, he also proceeded to arrest Kefa during the Feast of Matzot. ... ⁶ The night before Herod was planning to bring him out, Kefa was sleeping between two soldiers, who had him bound with two chains, and the guards standing at the door were in charge of the entire prison. ⁷ But the angel of יהוה *came to him, and the light illuminated the entire inside of the prison. He struck Kefa on the side to awaken him, and said, "Quick! Get up!" and the chains fell off his hands. ⁸ The angel said to him, "Get dressed and put on your sandals", and he did. Then he said to him, "Wrap your sash around your tallit and follow me."*

Acts 12v1-8

Second Occurrence

The second occurrence was in early August 2019 at Newark Liberty International Airport, New Jersey. This time as well, my wife and I booked a hotel near the airport for the night before our international family (with our children) trip, to avoid the last minute rush. The driving time from northern Virginia to Newark airport is roughly four hours. For many reasons, we were not able to travel and spend the night in the hotel as planned. On the day of the flight, while we were still in Northern Virginia, and about an hour before taking the road, it was broadcast that there was a major traffic jam of about three (3) hours delay on I-495/I-95 which is the fastest route to that airport. A quick math showed that by the time we get to the airport, the airline would have closed the boarding gate. We prayed and received the go ahead of Holy Spirit. Thus, we took the road and were driving twelve to fifteen miles over the speed limit until we meet the broadcast traffic jam.

We kept praying till the way opened through it for us. We drove almost at the same speed until we reached that airport. Noticeably, although we saw traffic police vehicles a couple of times, we were not stopped. The only time we stopped was near the airport, to refill the gas of the rental car. Upon arrival, I rushed to park the vehicle on the curbside with flashing lights on and ran with our passports to the counter of the airline. The flight attendants started closing the check-in lanes. However, they had NOT yet closed. Halleluyah! When they saw multiple passports I placed on the counter, they refused to check us in. I told them that check-in online was done but I had multiple suitcases to register. The manager replied with a sarcastic smile, "Sir., you cannot board this flight". By this time, my wife had reached the counter as well with our three kids. Her

How *He* Got Me Started

walk was a bit slow because this time too, she was pregnant. I pointed my family to the manager. He said, "Like I said, you cannot get on this flight. Just forget about this trip." At that moment, within me, Holy Spirit said, "you are flying".

I looked and saw behind the manager a gentleman standing. He was dressed in a white shirt with gray pants. He had a remarkable smile in his face with very white teeth. I left the manager with my wife and addressed this gentleman saying, "Hi Sir.!" He responded, "Hi! What can I do for you"? I said, "I need your help. I have multiple suitcases and computer bags to bring in from the car. I must also return the car to the rental, and make sure the manager checks-in my family on the current flight." He said, "I will help you. Let's go!" Back to the car, he quickly unloaded all the suitcases and took them to the manager and began checking them in. He even provided an extra bag for an overweight suitcase. Praise God! I returned to empty the car. He joined me a few minutes later and said, "You are good! Give me the car key. I will drop it for you. Go!" "What is your name, Sir.," I asked in rush. "Prince", he replied. "Thank you, Prince!" I said and took off running.

Once at the airline's check-in, I was surprised to see neither my wife nor our children, but only two flight attendants. A lady and a gentleman. All the lights were off. "Where are my wife and children?" I asked. The male flight attendant said, "They are checked-in. But you are staying. Here is your passport. You cannot make it". I raise the tone of my voice and said, "Who is that person who thought that he or she has the right to make such a decision for my family? Do you know that my wife is pregnant? Are you going to take care of those three young kids during this international flight? Do you know who my wife is?" Immediately, the female attendant said, "Sir.! Follow me! I will take you through the express lane." I looked! She had my passport in her hand and was walking very fast. Believe it or not, I did not touch my passport again, even through immigration, until she handed it over to me right before we boarded the plane with my wife and children whom we caught up with on our way. Praise Yehovah our God who does wonders! Halleluyah! He secured our road trip, shortened it, and sent angel Prince to assist us in the physical to take that flight.

How *He* Got Me Started

⁴⁰ *When he arrived at the place, he said to them, "Pray that you do not enter into temptation."* ⁴¹ *He withdrew from them about a stone's throw and kneeled down, and prayed,* ⁴² *Father, if you are willing, remove this cup from me! Nevertheless, not my will but yours be done."* ⁴³ *Then there an angel appeared to him from heaven and strengthened him.*

Luke 22v40-43

Caught Up In Heavenly Realm And Heard Angels Praising Yehovah

This event occurred mid-December 2011 in Northern Virginia. In my night sleep, I was in a vision and began hearing heavenly singing. It was very loud but awesome! I heard the words of the melody. The words were, "Lift His name higher!" One group of singing voices was like the lead. Anytime that group lead voices said, "Lift His name", I heard a responding group of voices saying "Higher" in such a loud tone that echoed like thousands and thousands of cymbals hit together twice. It was so awesome that I decided to record it. It was at that moment that I realized that I was in a vision. How? Because I moved to go and get my voice recorder. This move, unfortunately, woke me up!

Realizing that I just woke up from that awesome vision, I said, "No way! I am going back into it, right now!". Thus, I closed my eyes trying and hoping to be taken back in the vision. Unfortunately, it was not happening. To save the moment, I grabbed my phone which was within reach and sang the song myself and saved it! That was it! How awesome would that have been, if I could stay in my sleep in the vision and be able to physically turn on my recording device and capture the singing that was happening in the spiritual realms. For sure, it would have been beyond words to have a heavenly song playing on a physical recorder. I would cherish such opportunity again. As I am writing this testimony, I pray Father God Almighty, in the precious and awesome name of your Holy Lamb Yeshua, the Savior of all the creation and my big brother, give me to live this moment again on a permanent basis in the congregation of your servants and be able to capture a piece of it on a human recorder. I know that with You, *all* things are possible!

How *He* Got Me Started

² I know a man in union with the Messiah who fourteen years ago was snatched up to the third heaven; whether he was in the body or outside the body I don't know, God knows. ³ And I know that such a man — whether in the body or apart from the body I don't know, God knows — ⁴ was snatched into Gan-'Eden and heard things that cannot be put into words, things unlawful for a human being to utter.

2 Cor. 12v2-4 (CJB)

Part III

While Visiting Switzerland And Benin

A

Switzerland 2020

Prayed And Holy Spirit Moved On A Congregation For Hours

This event took place on February 17, 2020, while we (wife and children) were on a trip in Geneva, Switzerland. Ahead of the trip, my younger brother who is the pastor of a small congregation in Geneva, asked that I make room in our schedule to share a moment with them. We agreed that I will talk about Holy Spirit in connection with the Azusa Street Revival. I identified on YouTube the right video of the Azusa Street Revival documentary and sent it to them. On February 17, 2020, my family joined the congregation for the service. Together we watched the video documentary after which I did an exhortation. I stressed the need for us believers in Yeshua to continue seeking the Power of Holy Spirit and all the gifts that come with it to be effective witnesses of the

Good News.

After the exhortation, I said the closing prayer and handed over the microphone to my brother who was standing by my side. I closed my eyes because he started to pray as well. Right at that moment, I began hearing some noise around. I quickly opened my eyes. There, was a great surprise! A good one! Without laying of hands, Holy spirit had begun moving on His people. Many of them were on the floor. The pastor started going toward his members and praying for them individually. I stood in place in front of the congregation praying, speaking in tongues, praising Yehovah, praising Yeshua, praising Holy Spirit for the visitation.

It got so intense that at some point the Pastor lost his balance. With the microphone in his hand, he walked backward over twenty feet about, trying to regain his control. He finally gave up and landed on top of a member that was already on the floor. What a scene! I went and grabbed the microphone from his hand and continued ministering in prayer. Many were blessed, healed, and delivered. Halleluyah!

There was a particular lady that could not keep eye contact with me. She was hiding behind the chairs on the floor. I commanded her to come out from her hiding place. She crawled on the floor over twelve feet about and stopped at my feet. Her eyes and face were full of terror because of the manifestation of Holy Spirit on me that the evil spirits that were abusing her saw. I commanded them out of her, and she became well. Immediately, she stood up on her feet and started praising God. Halleluyah!

After some time, the pastor came back to himself. Got up from the floor. I gave him back his microphone. He ministered a bit more to his people and we finally closed the meeting. In all, to Yehovah our God Almighty, to Yeshua His Holy Lamb and our Savior, and to Holy

How *He* Got Me Started

Spirit our Comforting Counsellor be *all* the glory from generation to generation and forever! It is worth mentioning an interesting historical fact about the trip: just as our flight left the Swiss airspace on February 27, the Swiss aviation authorities closed the country to all inbound and outbound flights because of the Covid-19 pandemic alert. Days after we returned to the US, the FAA (Federal Aviation Administration) issued the same order and grounded all commercial flights, for the same reason: Covid-19 pandemic alert. Very interesting!

B

Benin 2021

Threatened A Threatening Drunker With The Name "Yeshua"

This event occurred in Benin in 2021 while we (wife and children) were on a trip. My children reminded me of it and asked me to add it to the book. During our stay, we went to a beach near the presidential palace to relax and enjoy the beautiful nature our God created for us. By default, we do not let any demon ruin our good time. And this would not be any different. I noticed that other beach-goers near us (my family) started moving away to a safe distance from a man that seemed to have reached their seating area. I took a better look and realized that the man was drunk and had a bottle of liquor in his hand. Unfortunately, the beach police were nowhere nearby. So, I kept my eyes on him.

After the drunker had scared other people away, he unexpectedly turned and started walking toward my family. I took note of it and understood that the spirits of drunkenness in the man are begging for some "slap". I advanced toward him while saying, "In the name of Yeshua! In the name of Yeshua! In the name of Yeshua!". The surrounding people were watching to see the looming confrontation. As I continued to advance decisively toward him, he suddenly changed his path and went away. I shouted praise Yehovah! My wife and children cheered up! Halleluyah!

How *He* Got Me Started

[17] *The seventy returned again with joy, saying, "Master, even the demons are subject to us through your name."* [18] *Yeshua said to them, "I saw hasatan come down out of the heavens like lightning [when you interfered with his subjects].* [19] *I gave you the authority to tread on serpents and scorpions, and authority over all the power of the enemy. Nothing shall by any means hurt you.* [20] *Notwithstanding, do not rejoice in that the spirits are subject to you, rather rejoice because your names are written in heaven."* [21] *In that hour Yeshua rejoiced, and prayed, "I thank you for hiding these things from the wise and prudent but revealing them to babes – for so it seemed good in your sight, O Father."*

Luke 10v17-21

Part IV

End Notes

End Notes

There are two spiritual occurrences relative to the completion of this book that you deserve to know. The first occurrence happened the night I finished writing the manuscript of the book, while the second occurrence happened the night I selected the cover page design of the book. I call them "bonus to the reader."

First Vision

This is a vision in my sleep during which I prayed so loud that it startled my household and woke me up. On May 09, 2024, I stayed overnight to complete the manuscript of the book. I went to bed a bit after 4:00 am. In my sleep, in the early hours of the morning, I was caught in a vision and my interaction in the vision was known to all my children who were in the next door bedroom. In the vision, I found myself in a fellowship with some brethren that I had neither any consciousness of having met before, nor any consciousness of race, gender, or skin color, except for the two main characters in the vision.

The fellowship was in a small wooden type of structure. It was full of peace and quiet. We were all listening to the Word of Yehovah. Nevertheless, no voice was speaking the Word that we were listening to. Suddenly, appeared in the room a man who walked toward the gathering. I could not clearly distinguish his physical appearance until the next scene. However, I knew he was present. He stated that he was there to arrest a man that was standing on the outer layer of the fellowship in the back.

Then, I saw this latter man walking away from the fellowship toward the former, with no resistance, whatsoever. His face seemed that of a black man. I sensed inside of myself that he was an innocent man. They both walked toward the exit door. It was then that I could see both men clearly. The one who came to arrest, was of high physical stature, dressed in a dark blue shirt. I saw his back, but not his face. However, the color of his appearance (neck and arm) was like aluminum dark. The man under arrest, was of a bit higher physical stature. He was wearing a leather-like sleeveless top that displayed his strong arms' muscles. His skin color was also like aluminum dark. Considering his physical body advantage, I told myself that he had what it takes to crush the first man and prevent being arrested.

As I was watching, he walked faster to reach the door and locked it up. I thought a serious fight was about to break out. He turned, and to my very big surprise, he stretched his hand, pointed at me and said, "You! Pray!" A deep groaning of anger arose inside of me for the trespassing of the fellowship to arrest this innocent man who also seems to be the owner of the fellowship. I blazed up in prayer. I remembered that I was rebuking the man who came to make the arrest. I said to him, "Even if you have the authority, why did you come here? Why did you dare trespassing this fellowship? Why have you come to arrest an innocent man?" I continued this raging prayer of protest and intercession for the man under arrest. It was so loud that the tone of my own voice woke me up a couple of times. I prayed in English and in French. One of my kids said that he heard one or two words in my native African language. The prayer became so intense that it started moving my body in the bed. I remembered that in one of the last portions of the prayer, I was urging the fellowship to *pray that our thoughts be kept secret from the Adversary.*

Then I felt the hands and voice of my three-year old girl touching my hand and talking to me. She had just come into the room. I said to her, "Abba is praying. Abba is praying. I had a vision". So, she left. I was still under the intensity of the vision and trying to recover my breath. My eyes were still closed. A few minutes later, her older sister came into the room. I asked her if she had heard me praying. "Yes! And very loud!", she replied. Then I told her that I was having a vision. She ran upstairs to tell her mother that I was praying loud in a vision. Her mother came down to the room thinking that I was already fully awake to chat, because she also heard me praying in an unusual way. Realizing the contrary, she tried to rush away. I called her back and told her to stay. Then, holding her hand, I prayed for her. It was around 8:00 AM in the morning. I did not know how long the vision lasted.

Later that same morning, I called our children to "investigate" what they heard. When I asked if they heard me praying early that morning, they started laughing, saying:

> *From our bedroom, we started to hear your voice getting louder. It became so loud that we thought we were making so much noise that we were disturbing your sleep. Therefore, we stopped playing and went very quiet. However, you did not stop. Then we began to hear words such as Yehovah, I pray, etc. Then, we understood that you were praying. But it was very loud!*

I told them that I had a vision. They asked what it was about. I gave them a quick insight and prayed for them. They will also read the full account in this book. What a vision! And what a prayer of intercession! I pray and ask you Holy Spirit, in the mighty and supreme name of Yeshua, to enlighten me about this vision at your will. Praise be to Yehovah our God Almighty and our Creator, from generation to generation and forevermore!

How *He* Got Me Started

Second Vision

This second event happened the night I selected the cover page design of this book. It was a spiritual attack during my sleep. I was in a vision and Holy Spirit told me that it was an attack. In the night of Thursday May 16, I went to bed for a much deserved sleep after a long day and spending the last hour on finalizing the selection of the cover page of this book. I was having a good sleep until I was caught in a vision. I saw that I was resting and not fully asleep. I was on the inner side of the bed. My wife was laying in the bed by my side. I also sensed that one or two of our young kids were sleeping in the lower part of the bed. It is a large bed. However, it is unusual for our kids to sleep in our bed at night.

Suddenly, appeared on the bedside a shape in the likeness of a young adult size person standing. The light was dimmed in the room in the vision, just as in reality. I could not clearly see the face. I thought it was one of our older kids 10-12 years old. I said, "You also want to join us here! OK! Come in!" The appearance did not make any sound. Nevertheless, when it bent over to slide in the bed between my wife and myself, I noticed that the appearance had no clothes on its human shape. At that moment, still in the vision, I heard the voice of Holy Spirit saying to me, "It is a demon."

I went on a raging counterattack prayer and the vision stopped. My eyes were opened. I charged on the Adversary in prayer. I issued a mandate of arrest of that particular demon and any other demon that might have been associated, in any way, with the attack. Any demon that might have EVEN just heard of the attack should also be arrested immediately. I ordered their arrest, torment, death and destruction. I ordered their bodies to be cut into pieces, set on fire and burnt completely like in Daniel chapter 7 verse 11. I kept that fighting attitude throughout that day, trusting that the power of Holy Spirit in the mighty and supreme name of Yeshua has already destroyed those attackers of my family.

When I woke up from the vision, it was very early Friday morning. My wife had already left our bed. However, there was neither kids in our bed nor had any of them slept in our bed that night. It was all a spiritual setup to lower my senses and attack. But thanks to Yehovah God for Holy Spirit our Comforting Counselor, who was watching over! He opened my spiritual eyes to see the attack through the vision and stop it. Praise be to Yeshua our Savior and Master who gave us authority and power over all the powers of the Adversary! Halleluyah! Praise be to Yehovah our Father and God from generation to generation and forevermore!

How *He* Got Me Started

¹ In days gone by, God spoke in many and varied ways to the Fathers through the prophets. ² But now, in the acharit-hayamim, he has spoken to us through his Son, to whom he has given ownership of everything and through whom he created the universe. ³ This Son is the radiance of the Sh'khinah, the very expression of God's essence, upholding all that exists by his powerful word; and after he had, through himself, made purification for sins, he sat down at the right hand of HaG'dulah BaM'romim. ⁴ So he has become much better than angels, and the name God has given him is superior to theirs.

Heb. 1v1-4 (CJB)

Acharit-hayamim. the end times
HaG'dulah BaM'romim": The Greatness on High (YeHoVah)

About the Author

Luc Nounagnon is a graduate in Banking and Finance, in Information Technologies, and in Management. He overflows with passion for the God of Israel and the Hebrew language. Luc Nounagnon was born to a modest Protestant Methodist family in the Republic of Benin (West Africa). He grew up in the capital city Cotonou where he attended school until graduating from university. After a couple of years of combined employment in the financial sector and volunteering work in Christian ministry, he migrated to the United States for further graduate studies.

He arrived in America in November 1999, right before the Y2K "madness", where he has since lived, studied, worked, conducted ministry, built a family, and created a business. The author spent some time in Lagos, Nigeria learning English, which later became an asset. French is used as the official language in Benin, along with other native languages. He has two new titles coming very soon. One of them is "Terumah". In it, the author unveils an antique secret of prosperity and riches for the benefit of the children of Yehovah and for the progressive manifestation of His kingdom through each individual life.

¹¹ *If a son shall ask bread of any of you that is a father, will he give him a stone (that looks like a loaf of bread)? If he asks for a fish, will he give him a serpent instead of a fish? ... ¹³ ... how much more shall your heavenly Father give the Ruach Ha Kodesh to those who ask him?*

Luke 11v11-13

How *He* Got Me Started

² *Suddenly there came a sound like a rushing mighty wind from heaven, and it completely filled the Beit HaMikdash, where they were sitting.* ³ *There appeared to them a pillar of fire, splitting apart and resting upon each of them,* ⁴ *and they were all filled with the Ruach HaKodesh and began to speak in other languages as the Ruach gave them the articulation ...* ⁶ *the multitude came ...* ⁷ *They were all amazed and marveled, saying, to each other, "Look! Are not all these men who are speaking Galileans?* ⁸ *Then how do we hear each of them speak in the dialects of the nations in which we were born?* ⁹ *Parthians, and Medes, ... Cappadocia, and Pontus, and Asia,* ¹⁰ *Phrygia, and Pamphylia, and Egypt, in the parts of Libya about Cyrene,...*

Acts 2v2-10

Beit HaMikdash: house of prayer

www.ingramcontent.com/pod-product-compliance
Lightning Source LLC
Chambersburg PA
CBHW060609080526
44585CB00013B/750